THE DO GOODERS

BE YOU

NAVEENPRASANTH

Contents

1. To The Strongest Girl- Raj kumari

*I may not share the last piece of
chocolate with you
But i will definitely share your
problems...
I may fight with you and not talk
To you for days, because my ego
mattered...
And now I realized yo cannot be
replaced with my ego
I wish to you tell you, "Don't
Leave, stay with me! : but your
Freedom is more important than
my wishes...
I may not tell you that I Love you
So much or do your favourites,
and you know what? My eyes
become teary when I see you
To talk about your perfection in
front of me...
I wish to be stronger, braver*

and to live not just survive.

2. Rain - Keerthi Thangamuthu

When clouds approach fast
Lightning lights it's flash
Thunders roll and crash,
Amidst the cloud's pry
And thuderclap's cry,
Tears roll down as Rain.

3. Agriculture - Keerthi Thangamuthu

Sown on the top
Tender that pop,
Crops are grown
On the land that is beocon,
Grows thin as tender
If not fed become slender,
Spreads itself and grow
Become useful to many.

4. Dreams - Keerthi Thangamuthu

Dreams helps us to cope
With the painful memories we have,
It gives a feeling of Confidence
To stand up and walk,
Washing out the feeling of being drained
Making the brain to recharge,
Experts believe in control of dreams
That seize all sorts of fantastic things,
It master's us in few ways
But success lacks in us,
Work with confidence
Till you reach the state,
Making our brain to exchange
Bringing success in your life.

5. Joy of nature - Sowbarnika Sry. AP

Flowers are delicate
Spreading fragrance everywhere
Attracting from miles away
Adorned in the feet of lord,
Expressed by many in the world
Bringing insects that are miles away.
Got its beauty from the mud
A moral to everyone's life
Spreading its beauty to miles away
Its fragrance fills us wherever we are,
By shedding its richness of purity
Refreshing our mind from miles away.

6. My special teacher -Sowbarnika Sry. AP

You touched my inner soul
The clarity you gave to me
Its shows like angel says
Like water rushed on golden sand,
And crashed along the bays
The questions deep within my heart,
Yet when you spoke your words aloud,
It seemed, no longer I was blind
The answers all came flooding in,
The knowledge that you gave to me
Within my heart, I hold,
I thank you, most graciously
These words I say aloud,
For you have changed my fate
And given me a bright future
Shedding tears I tell you,
"Good bye"

7. The Truth - Indhu

Conversations with you is,

The favorite part of my life.

You gather all sparkly words,

With all your heart and

You made me smile.

We always talk About us of,

Being the best and forever.

Till the earth summons us within,

We talk about us of

Contributing love forever.

The truth is you lied ,

By your sparkly words with all your heart.

You lied about us.

Oh you lied in returns ,

For all that I gave YOU.

8. Build Your Glittering Home -Indhu

Build your home with full of dreams,
Make it your own home, where
You manifest all your own hopes.
Don't let people come and go
Who don't care about
the chambers of your heart.
They are your only true home.
Don't turn your heart into a shelter of lost souls.
People come with dirty feet and;
Their mouths will leave you bleed.
Don't let your mind become a court
Of heartless beings.
They will satisfy their needs and;
Tear down your feelings.
They will laugh on your face
And disgrace behind your face.
You would have given your hole life
For these real monsters in disguise.
Don't le these monsters come and go

Into your glittering home.

9. Farming - NaveenPrasanth

Start each day with the belief that you can win the hearts of the next generation of farmers through love. Grandpa, do you know someone who loves farming?

The nicest place to be is on a farm; it's like going on a voyage; the moment was captured by live, and it was a bliss.

With love, laughter from, and your pleasures, farming makes the heart grin and works its magic.

I believe a strong light illuminated the farmers' faces, giving them hope that the people's hunger would be alleviated.

I most anticipated the circle of life, which is always a part of the farming field.

With love and hope, let's grin at the future and improve farming.

Grandpa, I hope your dream comes true. You are the best farmer I have ever known.

10. Hello, Fairy - NaveenPrasanth

*Because you are my queen and because you love me more than
my soul, I will give you a gentle kiss.
Princess, please do everything you can to help me feel at peace.
With you, Possible, u the magnificent, one cannot always be.
I'll never leave you, you're the strongest person here, at whatever
cost.
Tone makes worthy of Five after a break of five plus years.
Looking forward to a tone.*

11. Friend - NaveenPrasanth

I made a new friend, who at first knew nothing about me but later learned everything about me. I told her about the time I thought of her as my treasure.
Her eyes are like leaping fish, her brows are like a rainbow, her speech is my music, her words motivate me, and it is because of her that I am in the situation I am in today.
I miss her so badly right now.
We are still connected in my heart forever, despite the passage of time!

12. Childhood - NaveenPrasanth

Since I'm still in my childhood and that's still a part of you, I'm going to make a vow for tomorrow that I hope all of my dreams come true.

My life began with the affection you showed me, and I can still feel your love and care toward me.

I wouldn't be here without you both.

Despite my advanced age, you are always there to hear what I have to say.

Why ? your devotion to me.

No one can display love like you two, dear mother and pa.

I feel like you two are with me forever, so please don't leave me alone.

I'm going to make a promise for tomorrow, and I'm hoping that my dreams come true because I'm still young.

13. Farmer - NaveenPrasanth

Because he used to be a farmer, he believes in god.

He invokes God.

He sows the seeds on the ground and prays to God to bless it so that it would grow well.

He does most of the caring and is optimistic because of the recent rain.

the forehead with your hands

Go up and look at the sky; it is filled with rain for seed growth.

He cultivated the crops since he recognises the significance of rain and hopeful land.

As a farmer, my grandfather passed the farm to his son.

However, I adore my grand dad.

I wish to express my sincere gratitude to my grandparents, who have always lived with me.

I am holding one of the supporters in my hands while I pray that God would continue to bless them.

14. One to Love - NaveenPrasanth

Bring your loved one in.

If you love, don't accept a liar.

Prayer, which is magical between us, is my only hope.

Come and visit with me if you are in a position to.

Come in, my darling, and let's soar together on our golden wings!

Come in with love, not a liar! ready to receive you.

People might chuckle!

I won't pay them any mind, May. They then refer to me as different.

I was taught that if you enter, goodness is my beauty and I feel a good lover.

If you come in, I pray that my love will make both of us happy.

15. Hello, farmer-
NAVEENPRASANTH

Don't give up; the beginning is now.
Futures are coming, and they won't be destroyed. We have hope
that farming, soils, and seeds will advance.
Feature gives seeds life,
A seed can produce thousands of seeds, which will satisfy
beginners' appetite.
Greetings, Grandpa
Don't worry, I'll succeed in becoming a farmer like you with
Your help.
I wish futures were,
Ready to start farming, considering the need for extra, starter
seeds...

16. Waking Me - NAVEENPRASANTH

Dear nature, thank you for waking me up. The sky is a brilliant blue, and the sun was brighter than usual.
I can breathe freely, which makes me stronger and healthier. You are too great to contribute, not hurting nature.

You are preventing me from breathing.
If a weapon touches you, raise your hands in a gentle killing motion while killing with your spirit.
I'll vow that you are my true love and the parent of all living things, nature.

17. My Ship - NaveenPrasanth

I was never supposed to see or hear that name.
I started writing to express myself after I was heard.
ponders her name a lot,
Even my empty mind can be filled with a word.
She raises her hand and modifies my sign, making it more
attractive and adding a charm.
I felt more love for her than I had anticipated. This friendship
has just begun without any prior plans.
I gained a lot of knowledge. Still, thanks to her relationship, I
continue to learn a lot.
Others will be envious of both of us if she doesn't leave me too,
thus I won't leave her.

18. Patience - Amirtha

Don't lose patience
Be hopeful
Because soon the puzzle pieces
Will find it's designated places
Although sometimes it may take a while
And it seems that you are wasting your time
Know that it's worth it and not a wasting of time
Worthy things cannot be achieved easily
Patience is always the key to succeed...

19. Patience - Amirtha

Patience is not sitting and waiting,
It is foreseeing..
It is looking at the thorn and seeing the rose,
Looking at the night and seeing the day..
Successful people know that the moon
Needs time to become full...

20. Patience - Amirtha

Patience
and dream
Are like sun and like moon
Without ,
Patience our dream
Will remain in the dark..

21. Love - Amirtha

I live in his head
He thinks my thoughts
I finish his sentences
He knows my next move
This is how we love!!!

22. Hope - Amirtha

Hope is the place where I want to go..
Hope is the person who I want to know..
Hope is the feeling that carries me through..
Hope is the future for you and me....

23. Pain - Amirtha

The first few years of life is so painful..
The remaining years will also be painful..
But the pain is sweet ; because I'll always have you by my side....

24. Mom - ShubaPriya

She is not a princess
But a queen of my heart,
She is not an artist
But i am a fan of her,
She is not a star in the galaxy
But always glitters to my eyes,
She is not a god
But always safeguards me,
She is not an educationist
But always teaches me,
She is not a pathway
But always a mentor,
She is not a creator
But gave a birth to me,
Yeah, she is my
Mom...!

www.ingramcontent.com/pod-product-compliance
Lightning Source LLC
Chambersburg PA
CBHW061410160726
47995CB00002B/553